WE ♥ SON HEUNG-MIN

A GUIDE TO THE SOCCER SUPERSTAR

A catalogue record is available for this book from the British Library.
10 9 8 7 6 5 4 3 2 1
ISBN 978 1 83935 042 9

Printed and bound in China
Author: Emily Stead
Editor: Suhel Ahmed
Designer: Cloud King Creative
Design Manager: Sam James
Picture research: Paul Langan
Production: Gary Hayes

All facts and stats correct as of June 2020

WE ♥ SON HEUNG-MIN

A GUIDE TO THE SOCCER SUPERSTAR

MORTIMER

CONTENTS

MEET SON!

Welcome to this ultimate fan guide all about Asia's favourite footballer, Son Heung-min. In this book you'll discover fun facts, super stats and awesome pics of the soccer superstar!

Son Heung-min is the Tottenham Hotspur and Korea Republic forward who has the world at his feet. Since his move to Spurs, Son has taken the Premier League by storm, winning armies of fans from London to Seoul, thanks to his fun-loving personality and jaw-dropping goals.

Despite his global fame, his teammates describe Son as "one of the nicest people you'll ever meet", a player who remains down to earth and focused on his game. A true role model, the Korean is inspiring generations of young footballers around the world.

Want to know which are Son's greatest goals or what he likes to do when he's not pitchside? Read on to get to know the awesome icon that is Son Heung-min, then take the quiz to test your knowledge of Spurs' super No.7.

TURN THE PAGE TO KICK THINGS OFF!

Growing up, Son showed early promise as an athlete, demonstrating a talent for many sports. His father, Woong-jung, agreed to train Son and his older brother, Son Heung-yun, when they were old enough to show that they were serious about football. Woong-jung had been a professional footballer himself, and represented Korea Republic B team, but his career was cut short by injury. Determined not to let his sons suffer the same fate, Woong-jung took on the boys' training, and did not allow his sons to join a junior football club until they were teenagers.

1992 ➡

Son Heung-min is born on **8 July**, in **Chuncheon**, close to Korea Republic's capital, Seoul. His father is a former pro footballer who trains Son and his brother.

2006 ➡

Son begins to play competitive matches at youth level, **aged 14**.

Son's father, Woong-jung.

The brothers trained together, working on mastering ball control, dribbling and passing, while avoiding burnout. Their home schedule was still gruelling – the boys often completed six-hour training sessions, with up to four hours' straight of keepy-ups. Woong-jung's methods paid off, though, as Son is known for his fantastic technique and can shoot comfortably with both feet. Woong-jung now runs the SON Football Academy in the family's home city of Chuncheon, where the same training methods hope to uncover Korea Republic's next young football stars.

> **My father ... has done everything for me, and without him I probably wouldn't be where I am today.**
>
> **– SON HEUNG-MIN**

2008

He joins his first club, **FC Seoul** and later travels to Europe, aged 16, for a trial with **Hamburg**'s youth academy. Son formally joins the German club in 2009, after impressing at the **FIFA U-17 World Cup**.

2010

Earns his **first professional contract** with Hamburg, which he signs on his 18th birthday. The same year sees Son become a full international for **Korea Republic**.

2013

His talents earn him a move to the Bundesliga club, Bayer Leverkusen for €10 million, a then **club-record fee**.

RISING STAR

Son began his formal football career with FC Seoul, joining the club's youth academy in 2008. That same year, at the age of 16, the youngster left Seoul to team up with Hamburg SV's academy in Germany. A move to Europe at such a young age, and without knowing the language, was massive for Son, so his father made the trip overseas too.

2015 →
Signs for **Tottenham Hotspur** in a mega-money deal. The €30 million fee makes Son the most expensive Asian player in history.

2018 →
Son is given the captain's armband to lead Korea at the **2018 Asian Games**.

A young Son, starring for Hamburg's academy.

Son and van Nistelrooy, Hamburg teammates.

Son quickly settled in Germany, combining schoolwork with pre-season training. Training was less intensive than in Korea, and the young player's passion for football grew. By the summer of 2010 – his first year with the first team – Son was competing for a starting place with such seasoned pros as Ruud van Nistelrooy. A dream debut would soon follow...

To read more about Son's time at Hamburg, turn to pages 22-27.

2019

Son's status as a global superstar is confirmed as Spurs reach the **UEFA Champions League final** that year.

2020

Son shines while completing his **military service** in Korea, in the midst of the global lockdown due to coronavirus.

STAR
SHOT

"FOOTBALL IS MY HAPPINESS."

7 SUPER SON FACTS

1

Son began kicking a ball soon after learning to walk, and has loved football ever since. **"Football is in my blood,"** says Son.

2

As a ten-year-old he could do **keep-ups** for four hours without the ball touching the ground.

3

Growing up, Son dreamed of playing in the German **Bundesliga**. He joined Hamburg SV at 16, and switched to Bayer Leverkusen, aged 20.

5

He improved his German by watching German-language episodes of **SpongeBob SquarePants**!

6

Son still lives with his parents, in an apartment near Spurs' stadium in **Hampstead**, North London.

4

When Son moved to Europe, he thought people wouldn't be able to say his full name correctly, so called himself "**Sonny**." The nickname has stuck ever since!

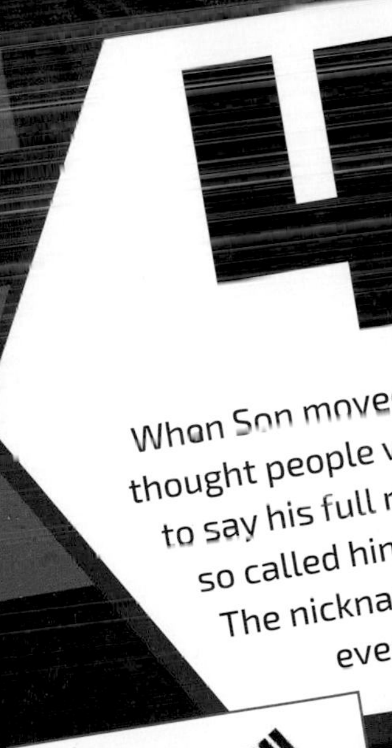

7

His role model is Juventus and Portugal legend **Cristiano Ronaldo**, because of the forward's work ethic.

SON'S SOCIALS

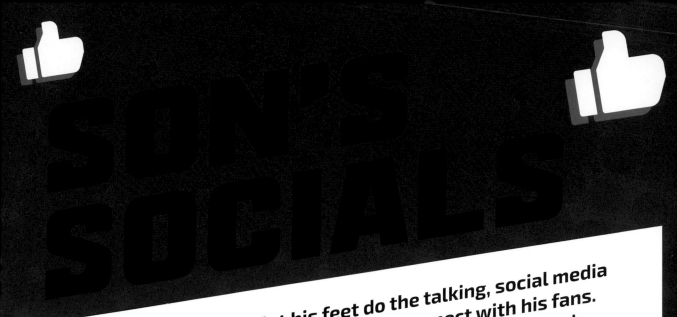

Although Son prefers to let his feet do the talking, social media offers the footballer the opportunity to connect with his fans. If you'd like to celebrate special moments in Son's life, here's how to follow his official social media channels.

INSTAGRAM
@hm_son7
4 million+ followers

FACEBOOK
(In Korean)
@HeungMinSonOfficial
1 million+ followers

For all the latest match action, news and gossip, you can also check out:

TOTTENHAM HOTSPUR

Twitter & Instagram
@SpursOfficial

@spursofficial

KOREA FA

Korea Football Association
Twitter & Instagram
@theKFA

@hm_son7 collects the Premier League Goal of the Month award in December 2019 for his stunner against Burnley.

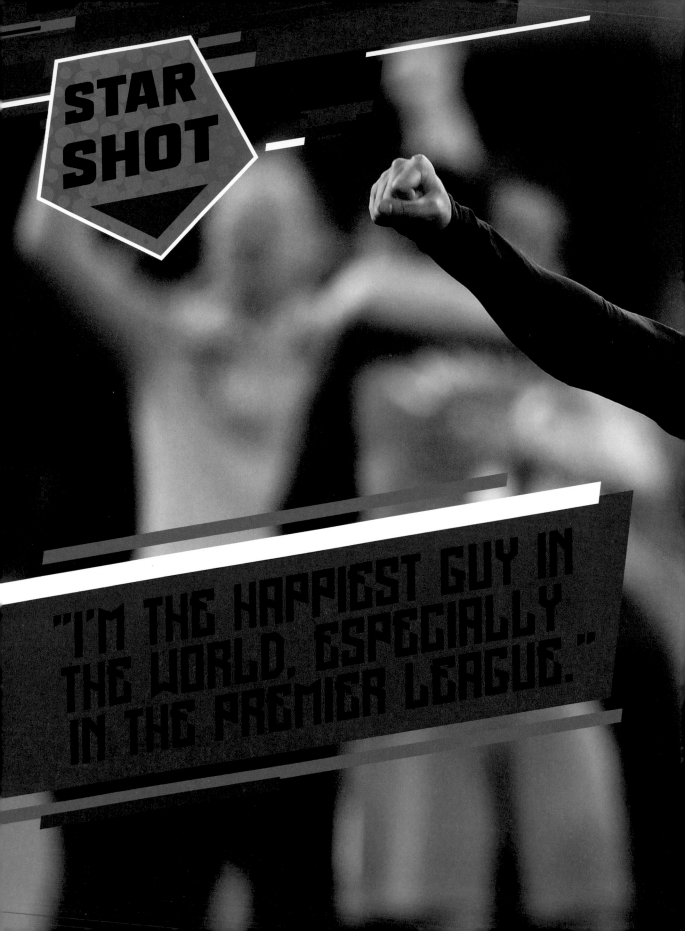

STAR SHOT

"I'M THE HAPPIEST GUY IN THE WORLD, ESPECIALLY IN THE PREMIER LEAGUE."

HAMBURG SV

Son's move to Hamburg SV, aged 16, was arranged following a deal between the Korea Republic FA and the Bundesliga club. Three trialists trained with Hamburg's youth academy, but only Son showed special promise and went on to sign a pro contract with the club.

SETTLING IN

Son's eagerness to learn the German language saw him quickly adapt to life in a new country. Taking lessons helped Son become fluent in super-fast time and the teenager established himself as a favourite among the Hamburg players and staff early on.

Joined: November 2009

Stadium: Volksparkstadion

Nicknames: *Die Rothosen* (The Red Shorts), *Der Dino* (The Dinosaur)

Fly Emirates

APPS: 78

SQUAD NUMBERS: 15 & 40

GOALS: 20

Rafael van der Vaart is the first to congratulate Son, after the Korean strikes twice against Borussia Dortmund in 2012.

Son was a happy Hamburger!

HAMBURG SV
THE MANAGERS

Son played under a string of managers while at Hamburg SV, with each one impressed by Son's commitment and technique. His promotion from the youth team was rapid, and Son was drafted into the first-team squad for the 2010-11 season.

ARMIN VEH

Son was very much in manager Armin Veh's plans at the start of the 2010-11 season, following an impressive pre-season. As soon as his fitness allowed, Son was given his first-team debut.

Veh was delighted to have uncovered such a "gem of a striker" and first played Son in a German Cup match against Eintracht Frankfurt on 27 October, 2010.

Son's first goal for the club came three days later, on his Bundesliga debut, against FC Köln. Veh was impressed by the youngster's mature performances and more first team appearances followed.

66 At 18 years of age, Son can already do so much that others at 30 years of age can't. 99
– ARMIN VEH

THORSTEN FINK

Fink became Son's coach in October 2011, at a time when Hamburg were at the foot of the Bundesliga table, desperate to survive relegation and hold on to their star players. Fink worked on Son's positioning, freeing him up to score key goals, which helped save Hamburg from the drop.

The following season, Son scored 12 goals. His best performances came against Jürgen Klopp's Borussia Dortmund, the league's defending champions, as Son scored doubles in both fixtures.

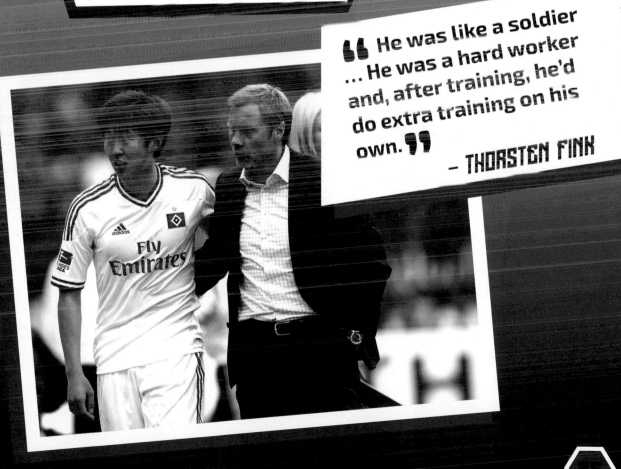

66 He was like a soldier ... He was a hard worker and, after training, he'd do extra training on his own. **99**

— THORSTEN FINK

How many of these eight fab facts do you know from Son's seasons at Hamburg?

1

After starring in the **FIFA U-17 World Cup** in 2009, Son turned down Blackburn Rovers and Portsmouth in England, to stay with Hamburg.

2

His 18th birthday was made extra special, when Hamburg handed Son his **first senior football contract** that same day.

3

Son scored his **first Bundesliga goal** aged 18, making him Hamburg's youngest ever league goalscorer.

4

His teammate, former Dutch and Man United star **Ruud van Nistelrooy**, predicted a bright future for Son.

5 In the 2011-12 season, Son **scored the winner** against Hannover, ensuring Hamburg escaped relegation from the Bundesliga.

6 Son's teammates nicknamed him **"BVB Schreck"** (Borussia Dortmund's bogeyman) as he had a knack of scoring against the 2012 German champions.

7 Son left Hamburg in June 2013 to follow his dream of playing in the **UEFA Champions League**.

8 He would return to haunt Hamburg in his first match against his former club, scoring a **hat-trick** for Bayer Leverkusen in November 2013.

FAMOUS FRIENDS

Unlike some more showy footballers, Son prefers to keep a low profile. That's not to say that he doesn't attract famous friends and admirers! Check out which stars are happy to be linked with the friendly footballer...

Son and BTS are huge stars with global followings.

BTS

When K-pop sensations BTS were playing the British leg of their tour at Wembley Stadium in 2019, band member RM wore a cap emblazoned with "SON". Their opening night coincided with Spurs playing the biggest match of their history – the Champions League final against Liverpool. During the show, RM pointed to his cap, rapping, "I'm a new hero, Anpanman!" Word reached the flattered Spurs star, who announced himself as BTS's newest fan!

DAVID BECKHAM

Retired England star David Beckham and Son share many similarities – both became icons in their respective countries, and showed their determination to succeed in football by putting in extra hours on the training pitch. The pair keep in touch as Becks is an ambassador at Tottenham. Former Spurs boss Pochettino was right when he dubbed Son the "Beckham of Asia".

Becks and Son's favourite shirt is No.7 and they both love Korean food, too!

RYU JUN YEOL

A scene in the film star Ryu Jun Yeol's movie *Money* shows his character cheering on Son, while playing for Spurs. The pair have met in real life, too, and formed a close friendship, as they both share a love of the beautiful game. Son and Ryu may star in different industries, but they support each other's careers.

Ryu is one of Korea's brightest young movie stars.

COOL CARS

While Son remains focused on his football, the one thing he splashes the cash on are flashy cars! Petrolhead Son owns a collection of luxury motors worth over £1.5 million. Here's how the superstar likes to roll…

MASERATI LEVANTE

Son was gifted a gunmetal grey Levante by the Maserati owners, who said that Son and the car share the same unstoppable power! The Levante is Son's favourite SUV.

AUDI R8 COUPE

Often spotted behind the wheel of a sleek white R8 when in Korea, this speedy motor is sure to get the captain to international training camps on time!

FERRARI LAFERRARI

Just 499 of these exclusive supercars were produced – and Son owns one of them! He wisely chose black over classic red, the colour of Spurs' rivals, Arsenal. This model speeds from 0–60 mph in 2.9 seconds and can reach a top speed of 227 mph – though Son has never tested this!

RANGE ROVER

If you don't own a black Range Rover, are you even a Premier League footballer? Red leather sports seats and a classy matte black finish add extra bling to Son's 4x4.

BENTLEY CONTINENTAL GT

With its 6-litre twin-turbocharged W12 engine, Son's classic black Bentley revs from 0–60 mph in 4.3 seconds and has a top speed of 198 mph. A sweet ride!

STAR SHOT

"I TRY MY BEST, AND I WANT TO HELP MY TEAMMATES EVERY GAME."

CLUB PROFILE:
BAYER LEVERKUSEN

Having made a flying start in Europe with Hamburg, Son found himself on the radar of some of the bigger Bundesliga clubs. It was Bayer Leverkusen who won the race for Son's signature, in a €10 million deal, a move which saw the winger play in the UEFA Champions League for the first time, aged 20.

FAN CLUB

Son's arrival at Bayer brought new fans to the club from the large Korean community in the city. Many fans would queue for hours after matches for an autograph or signed shirt, with Son's mum and dad on hand to help take the photos. The Korean's popularity was beginning to soar...

Joined: June 2013

Stadium: BayArena

Transfer fee: €10 million

Nickname: *Die Werkself*
(The Company's Eleven)

APPS: 87

SQUAD NUMBER: 7

GOALS 29

Son opened his Champions League goal-scoring account in August 2014, a year after joining Bayer.

Bayer fans adored Son's spectacular goals and his trademark smile.

BAYER LEVERKUSEN
THE MANAGERS

Son's transfer to Bayer was masterminded by the club's sporting director and former German World Cup winner, Rudi Völler. Impressed by Son's maturity and finishing ability at a young age, Völler saw the winger as a key player in the club's future.

SAMI HYYPIA

Son flourished under Finnish boss, Sami Hyypia, who kept up the player's confidence following a goalless run of matches in his first season. Son bounced back with a hat-trick against his former club, Hamburg, one of his best matches for Bayer. Hyypia left the club in April 2014 after two years in charge.

ROGER SCHMIDT

Roger Schmidt was Son's next permanent coach at Bayer, joining for the 2014-15 season. The Korean was in explosive form that season, finishing as the club's top scorer and helping Bayer to reach the round of 16 in the UEFA Champions League, scoring five goals. At the start of the following campaign, though, Son was ready for the next challenge in his career – a move to the English Premier League.

66 [Son] is growing in stature and is becoming a lot more consistent. He has a lot of potential so I can only show my admiration for him. 99
– ROGER SCHMIDT

BAYER LEVERKUSEN
FAST FACTS

How many of these facts and stats from Son's time as a Bayer player did you know?

1 Upon signing for Bayer, Son followed in the footsteps of national hero **Cha Bum-kun**, the first South Korean to play in the Bundesliga.

2 He was handed the **number 7 jersey**, a squad number he kept at Spurs.

4 Son's goals tally reached **double figures** in the Bundesliga in both full seasons with Bayer.

3 The Korean struck a **hat-trick** in a 5-3 win over his former club in November 2013.

5 Fellow countryman **Ryu Seung-woo** was also on the books while Son was at Bayer.

6 Son shone in Europe in Bayer's 2014-15 UEFA Champions League campaign, **scoring five times**.

7 Bayer qualified for the **UEFA Champions League** in both of the full seasons in which Son played for the club.

8 He left the club in August 2015, having scored **29 goals in 87 appearances** – a fine return for a winger.

SIGNS YOU ARE A SON SUPERFAN

You've followed Son's journey from the Bundesliga to the Premier League, but just how much do you know about the Korea Republic hero? Here are eight signs that you're a total Son Heung-min superfan!

 1 You can reel off all Son's career stats so far – for each one of his clubs, as well as the national side!

 2 You have replayed every one of Son's TV interviews and read every magazine article about him… whether in Korean or English!

3 Whenever you chat football with your mates, you find any excuse to sneak Son into the conversation.

 4 You're just as interested in Son's life off the pitch as on it, and know all the cool stuff the forward enjoys when he's not playing… from food to music to films!

5 You've got the skills! Your signature goal when playing football with your friends is a strike from distance, just like your idol!

6 You've joined at least one fan group dedicated to the Spurs star on social media, so you always get the gossip first!

7 Your wardrobe contains at least one Tottenham top, a Hamburg or Bayer Leverkusen shirt, plus a Korea Republic strip with Son's name and number printed on the back.

8 Watching Son lift the Champions League trophy or the World Cup one day would be your ultimate dream!

Test your knowledge of the soccer superstar on page 76.

SON'S DREAM DOZEN

Son Heung-min has scored some sensational strikes for club and country. Here are 12 of his very best. How many do you remember? Look them up online, then rate each great goal out of five.

MY RATING:

BAYER LEVERKUSEN
v Zenit St Petersburg

UEFA Champions League November 2014
A brilliantly worked free kick saw Son pick up the ball from 30 yards and smash home.

KOREA REPUBLIC
v Australia

AFC Asian Cup January 2015
Son's extra-time left-foot strike levelled the scores in the Asian Cup final.

MY RATING:

Watford v TOTTENHAM HOTSPUR

FA Premier League December 2015
A cheeky backheeled flick with a minute to go sealed three away points for Spurs!

MY RATING:

Middlesbrough v TOTTENHAM HOTSPUR

FA Premier League September 2016
Superb solo work and a smart finish from the edge of the box made this a special goal.

MY RATING:

SON'S DREAM DOZEN

**TOTTENHAM HOTSPUR
v Swansea City**

**FA Premier League
December 2016**
Son's brilliant half-volley gave the Swansea keeper no chance.

MY RATING:

**Leicester City
v TOTTENHAM HOTSPUR**

**FA Premier League
May 2017**
Silky skills, a classy stepover and a fine long-range strike make this a mega Son goal.

MY RATING:

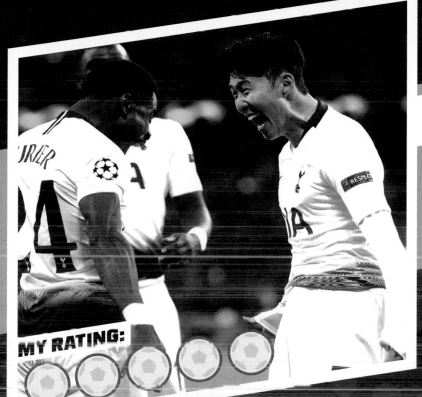

Borussia Dortmund
v TOTTENHAM HOTSPUR

UEFA Champions League
September 2017

A fine individual run and strike saw Son make the net bulge after just four minutes.

MY RATING:

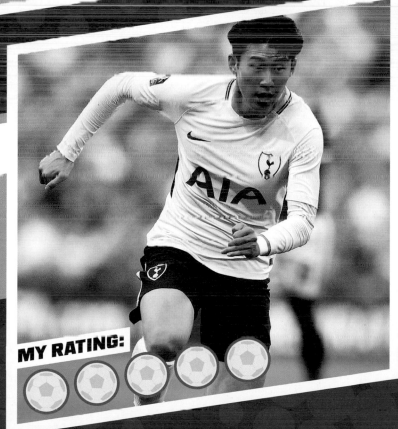

TOTTENHAM HOTSPUR
v West Ham United

FA Premier League
January 2018

An absolute screamer of a shot that found the top corner against the Hammers!

MY RATING:

SON'S DREAM DOZEN

KOREA REPUBLIC
v Germany

FIFA World Cup
June 2018
Son tapped into an empty net to seal Germany's exit from the 2018 World Cup in France.

MY RATING:

Leicester City
v TOTTENHAM HOTSPUR

FA Premier League
December 2018
This ball was bent brilliantly into the back of the net. A classic Son strike!

MY RATING:

Manchester City
v TOTTENHAM HOTSPUR

**UEFA Champions League
April 2019**
A quality finish with Son's favoured right foot sent the Spurs fans wild at the Etihad!

MY RATING:

TOTTENHAM HOTSPUR
v Burnley

**FA Premier League
December 2019**
A roving run from inside his own half and slick strike is one of Son's top career goals.

MY RATING:

TOTTENHAM HOTSPUR

The 2020-21 season is Son's sixth season with London club Tottenham Hotspur. He has a fantastic relationship with the players and coaching staff, and he is adored by the Spurs fans. When the time eventually comes to hang up his boots, it's clear that the club will forever be a part of Son's heart.

TOP STADIUM

Spurs moved to their new ground, the Tottenham Hotspur Stadium in April 2019. With a capacity of over 62,000, it's the second-largest stadium in the Premier League. Son enjoys the state-of-the-art facilities, which include an incredible curved dressing room complete with an ice bath!

Joined: Aug 2015

Stadium: Tottenham Hotspur Stadium

Transfer fee: €30 million

Honours: UEFA Champions League 2018–19 (runners-up)
Nicknames: Spurs, the Lilywhites

APPS: 220+

SQUAD NUMBER: 7

BEST MATES

Son is one of the most popular members of the Spurs' squad, thanks to his "Sonny" character. His fluent English and permanent smile make the forward easy to get along with.

Son's Spurs teammates have a whole lot of love for their Korean friend.

Son has a special bond with England midfielder, Dele Alli. The pair love to celebrate together when either player scores!

Like Son, defensive midfielder Eric Dier moved countries to join Spurs. Son greets Dier with a special handshake each day at training.

TOTTENHAM HOTSPUR
THE MANAGERS

Son has played under two different coaches since joining Tottenham. Both admire Son's strong work ethic and commitment to the team, making the forward one of the first names on Spurs' team sheet.

> **" He never gives up – he tries, tries, tries, tries. "**
> **– MAURICIO POCHETTINO**

MAURICIO POCHETTINO

Former Spurs manager Mauricio Pochettino showed great faith in Son when he signed the forward on a mega-money deal. After winning a starting place in Pochettino's side, Son went on to flourish under the Argentine, playing some of the best football of his career so far, as Spurs reached the UEFA Champions League final in 2018-19. When Pochettino left the club the following season, Son took to Instagram to thank his manager, saying,

"I have learned a lot from you, not only in football, but in life."

JOSE MOURINHO

When Jose Mourinho was appointed Spurs manager in November 2019, he arrived at the club having won the UEFA Champions League with two different clubs, as well as multiple Premier League and La Liga titles. Son was excited to be working with a manager who shares his own winner's mentality, while Son's wonder goals have impressed the boss.

"My son calls him Sonaldo Nazario!"
— JOSE MOURINHO

51

CLUB PROFILE:
TOTTENHAM HOTSPUR
FAST FACTS

Check out eight super Spurs facts that every Son fan should know!

1

Son's transfer fee of **£22 million** from Bayer Leverkusen made him the most expensive Asian player ever!

2

October 2015 saw Son win his first Premier League Player of the Month award, the **first Asian player** to do so. He won it again in April 2017.

4

The forward entered the history books by scoring the **first ever goal** at Spurs' new stadium. It came in a Premier League match against Crystal Palace in April 2019.

3

Son was handed the famous **no.7 shirt**, a shirt previously worn by Spurs legends, Ossie Ardiles and Steve Perryman.

5

Another honour won with the club was **Spurs' Goal of the Decade** for his incredible solo strike over Burnley in December 2019.

6

2018-19 was Son's strongest season with Spurs so far, as he netted **20 goals** in all competitions and made **ten assists**.

7

Son's **50th Premier League goal** for the club came in February 2020. A rebound from a penalty was one of his scrappier goals!

8

He's the **highest-scoring Asian footballer** ever to have played in English football.

FAN FEVER

Son has formed a close bond with his fans wherever he has played from Hamburg to Tottenham. The special player is always happy to sign shirts and pose for selfies with the faithful supporters who follow his career – nothing is too much trouble for Son!

> **❝ I want to make sure I make everyone happy by playing at the top level… to pay back to [the fans]. This is very important for me. ❞**
>
> **– SON HEUNG-MIN**

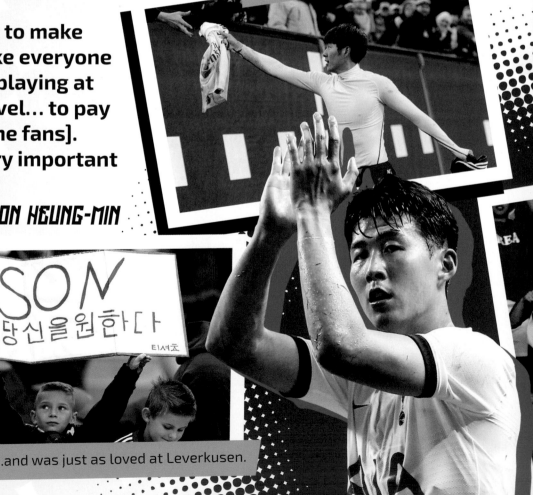

Son reached hero status at Hamburg…

SON
난 당신을 원한다
티셔츠

…and was just as loved at Leverkusen.

Korean fans have flocked to watch Son play in London ever since he joined Spurs, with many making a 10,000-mile trip from Korea Republic to watch their idol in action. Watching Son's matches on TV is a challenge for Korean fans back home, too, as a 3 p.m. kick-off in the UK means it's midnight in Korea. When he plays in the UEFA Champions League at 8 p.m., Korean fans must set their alarms for 5 a.m.!

Son greets a crowd of Korean fans.

PRIDE OF ASIA

Captain Son is a national treasure.

When Son returns to his home country to play for Korea Republic he's always mobbed by fans whose dream it is to meet the star in person. Son has become bigger than football – he's the country's biggest celebrity and his face is splashed on billboards and magazine covers at every turn. YouTube channels are dedicated to the Spurs man, while a nightly TV show called *Super Son Time* draws a huge audience.

OFF THE PITCH

After playing or training, Son needs his body to recover quickly. Here are some of the ways he likes to relax away from the football pitch and gym.

Son has styled his north London home with a minimal look.

MOVIE NIGHTS

Son would much rather hang out at home watching Korean movies than be snapped at a swanky London nightclub late in the early hours... much to the delight of his managers!

Korean K-Pop heroes, BTS.

Bang Min-ah of Korean girl group, Girls Day.

TOP TUNES

Son loves listening to Korean music, even though most of his teammates have never heard of any of the bands! Some of his hip hop favourites might just make the dressing room playlist, though. He's friends with the K-Pop wonders, BTS, and is rumoured to have dated the Korean pop stars, Bang Min-ah and Yoo So-young in the past, too.

FAVE EATS

Son loves healthy food from home, made by his mum, especially Korean rice dishes and barbecue. He's often spotted having a family meal at the Korean restaurant You Me, in south London.

Korean barbecue is Son's absolute fave!

KOREA REPUBLIC

Son won his first cap for his country in December 2010, aged 18. He has played at two FIFA World Cups, the 2018 Asian Games, three AFC Asian Cups and the 2016 Olympic Games in Rio. Son was given the honour of captaining the Asian Tigers in 2018 and has become one of the most important players in the nation's history.

Debut: 30 December, 2010

Stadium: Seoul World Cup Stadium

Honours: Asian Games 2018, Asian Cup 2015 (runner-up)
Nicknames: The Tigers of Asia, The Taeguk Warriors

Son tasted gold with Korea Republic at the Asian Games in 2018.

CAPS:
87

SQUAD NUMBER:
7

GOLDEN GAMES

Son was selected as one of the under-23 squad's three overage players for the 2018 Asian Games. It was during the tournament that Son captained the Taeguk Warriors for the first time. His two assists in the final saw Korea Republic beat Japan 2-1 in extra time to clinch the gold medal. The victory also saw the length of Son's military service reduced.

Son in action during the Asian Games' gold-medal match against rivals Japan.

KOREA REPUBLIC
TEAM HIGHLIGHTS

SUPER SKIPPER

Son has captained his country since 2018. His mature character, relaxed nature and strong values are an ideal blend to lead the team. Son always gives 100% on the pitch and commands the respect of his team-mates and opponents, as well as the media.

On captain duties before the World Cup 2022 qualifier against Lebanon.

Son leads by example on the training ground.

The Korea captain always looks the part when representing his country.

TIGER KING

Paulo Bento was appointed Korea Republic manager in 2018 and is tasked with taking the Tigers to the 2022 FIFA World Cup in Qatar. Set to be Son's third World Cup tournament, Korea's captain will play a key part in qualification.

INTERNATIONAL PROFILE:
KOREA REPUBLIC
FAST FACTS

Heung-min has been a Son-sational performer for his country – check out his accomplishments!

1
Son's debut goal for Korea Republic came at the **2011 AFC Asian Cup** in a 4-1 victory over India.

2
He scored a 90th-minute equalizer in the **2015 AFC Asian Cup final**, but Korea lost out to eventual champions, Australia.

4
Son has also represented Korea at an **Olympic Games** in 2016, but suffered a shock defeat to Honduras in the quarter-finals.

3
He's played and scored at **two FIFA World Cups** – Brazil 2014 and Russia 2018.

5 Son is often likened to the country's goal king, **Cha Bum-kun**, but humbly plays down the comparisons.

6 He scored in the Tigers' famous victory over Germany, which eliminated the defending champions from the **2018 FIFA World Cup**.

7 The winger has his sights set on joining Korea's **top ten all-time scorers** and reaching 100 international caps.

8 If selected, the **2022 FIFA World Cup** in Qatar would make a hat-trick of tournaments for the star forward.

TRUE COLOURS

Take a look at some of the kits that Son has worn – which ones do you rate? Rank them in order, both home and away.

HAMBURG
Our hero rocking Hamburg's home strip.

BAYER LEVERKUSEN
Bayer's red and white kit was the business!

KOREA REPUBLIC
Son was born to wear the red and black of the Tigers of Asia.

TOTTENHAM HOTSPUR
Looking Son-sational as a Spurs' Lilywhite.

HOME

AWAY

HAMBURG
This navy number was a Bundesliga beauty!

BAYER LEVERKUSEN
Bayer's boy in black, looking slick.

KOREA REPUBLIC
Wearing white for a World Cup qualifier away from home.

TOTTENHAM HOTSPUR
Kitted out in navy for the Champions League.

SERVING HIS COUNTRY

Whether it's on or off the pitch, Son Heung-min gives his all when representing his country. The forward couldn't be prouder of his Korean roots – he considers being a role model for young people back home to be a special honour.

MILITARY MAN

In spring 2020, Son returned to Korea Republic to recover from a broken arm. The 2019-20 season was then impacted by the coronavirus pandemic, which saw football leagues around the world suspended. This period gave Son the chance to complete his national service, as the footballer began a three-week stint of military training.

Son delivered an outstanding performance for his country, shining at shooting and bayonet skills, individual battle skills and first aid.

SHARP SHOOTER

Son excelled at shooting and was named the top performer among 157 trainees. He graduated at a ceremony on the island of Jeju, winning the Pilsung prize.

STAR SHOT

"I'M ALWAYS HUNGRY. I CAN BE BETTER ALWAYS."

FUTURE GOALS

Son is an ambitious but humble player who always strives to perform well and help his teammates in every game. Here are the team and individual trophies on which Son has set his sights.

TEAM AWARDS

CHAMPIONS LEAGUE

It's no secret that Son would love to win the UEFA Champions League, having come so close to glory in 2018-19. Spurs reached the final following an epic semi-final win over Ajax, earning Son a runners-up medal, as Liverpool were crowned champions.

PREMIER LEAGUE

Son and Tottenham enjoyed their best Premier League finish in 2016-17, finishing second under Pochettino. Since then, Spurs have a new boss, as well as a spectacular new stadium. Winning the Premier League, one of the strongest leagues in world football, remains one of Son's top ambitions.

ASIAN CUP 2023

With the AFC Asian Cup set to take place in 2023 in China, Son will be 30 and at his peak. Son and Korea Republic came closest to winning the cup in 2015, losing in extra time in the final. Nothing would make Son prouder than to lift the trophy as captain.

INDIVIDUAL AWARDS

BALLON D'OR

In 2019, Son received his first nomination for the prestigious Ballon d'Or prize, awarded to the best male player in world football. With Cristiano Ronaldo and Lionel Messi approaching the twilight of their careers, could Son continue his remarkable rise to the top and become the first Asian player to win the award?

THE BEST FIFA MEN'S PLAYER

Making the ten-man shortlist for the Best FIFA Men's Player award would be a fitting reward for Son's progress in the game. As his profile in world football grows, Son could earn his first nomination for the award and send his fans wild!

ULTIMATE SON QUIZ

You've read this fans' guide to Son Heung-min, now it's time to see how closely you've been paying attention! Take the ultimate Son quiz to test your knowledge. Score one goal for each correct answer.

1 With which Korean club did Son begin his career?

A Jeju United ☐
B FC Seoul ☐
C Pohang Steelers ☐

2 What is Son's favourite meal?

A pizza ☐
B Korean food ☐
C vegetarian ☐

3 Which England star is not a Spurs team-mate?

A Eric Dier ☐
B Dele Alli ☐
C Raheem Sterling ☐

4 Which of these cool cars does Son not own?

A Lamborghini Huracan ☐

B Maserati Levante ☐

C Range Rover ☐

5 Which Bundesliga club has Son not played for?

A Hamburg ☐

B Borussia Dortmund ☐

C Bayer Leverkusen ☐

6 How many siblings does Son have?

A one ☐

B two ☐

C three ☐

7 How many international goals has Son scored for Korea?

A 0-10 ☐

B 10-20 ☐

C 20-40 ☐

8 Who did Son and Tottenham lose to in the UEFA Champions League final in 2019?

A FC Barcelona ☐

B Juventus ☐

C Liverpool FC ☐

Check your answers on page 80, then shade out a football for each question you got right.

AWARDS & NOMINATIONS

2010 ★ Bundesliga Young Player of the Hinrunde (half-season)

2013 ★ Korean Footballer of the Year

2014 ★ Best Footballer in Asia
★ Korean Footballer of the Year

2015 ★ AFC Asian Cup: Team of the Tournament
★ AFC Asian International Player of the Year
★ Best Footballer in Asia
★ Korean Goal of the Year

2016 ★ Korean Goal of the Year
★ Premier League Player of the Month (September)
★ The Asian Awards Outstanding Achievement in Sports

2017
★ AFC Asian International Player of the Year
★ Best Footballer in Asia
★ Korean Footballer of the Year
★ Premier League Player of the Month (April)

2018
★ AIPS ASIA Best Asian Male Athlete
★ Best Footballer in Asia
★ Bundesliga Hamburger SV All-time XI
★ Korean Goal of the Year
★ PFA Fans' Premier League Player of the Month (January)
★ Premier League Goal of the Month (November)
★ Tottenham Hotspur Goal of the Season (2017-18)

2019
★ AFC Asian International Player of the Year
★ Ballon d'Or nominee
★ Best Footballer in Asia
★ FIFA FIFPro World 11 nominee
★ Korean Footballer of the Year
★ London Player of the Year (2018-19)
★ Premier League Goal of the Month (December)
★ Tottenham Hotspur Goal of the Season (2018-19)
★ Tottenham Hotspur Player of the Season (2018-19)
★ UEFA Champions League team of the Group Stage (2019-20)

2020
★ BBC Premier League Goal of the Season (2019-20)*

*season to date

CARLING
Goal of
the Month

ANSWERS

ULTIMATE SON QUIZ

1. B – FC Seoul

2. B – Korean food

3. C – Raheem Sterling

4. A – Lamborghini Huracan

5. B – Borussia Dortmund

6. A – one

7. C – 20-40

8. C – Liverpool FC

PICTURE CREDITS